*a young pianists' first*

# BIG NOTE
# SOLOS

## 10 Original Compositions

*by William Gillock*

ISBN 978-1-4803-2141-0

Exclusively Distributed By

WILLIS MUSIC

HAL•LEONARD®
CORPORATION
7777 W. BLUEMOUND RD. P.O. BOX 13819
MILWAUKEE, WISCONSIN 53213

Visit Hal Leonard Online at
**www.halleonard.com**

# CONTENTS

**5**    Clowns

**14**    The Glass Slipper

**3**    Let's Waltz

**8**    The Little Shepherd

**13**    New Roller Skates

**6**    Pagoda Bells

**4**    Smoke Signals

**12**    Spooky Footsteps

**10**    Swing Your Partner

**9**    Water Lilies

# LET'S WALTZ

WILLIAM GILLOCK

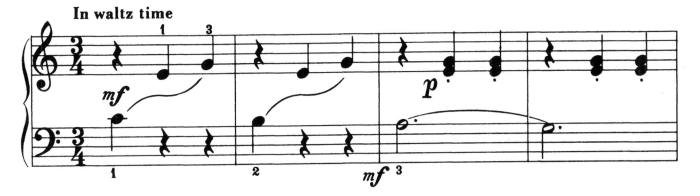

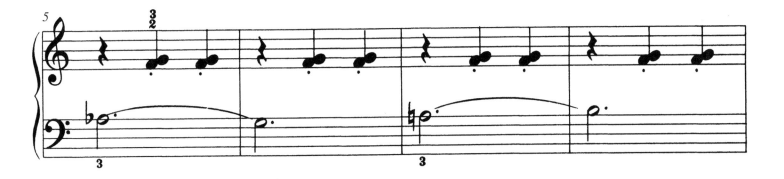

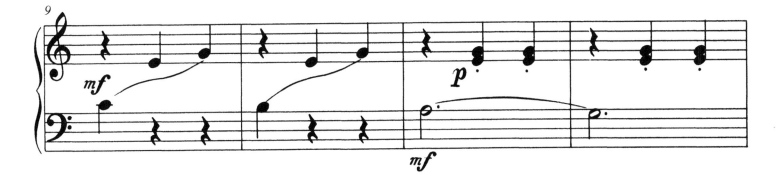

# SMOKE SIGNALS

WILLIAM  GILLOCK

**Steadily, with marked rhythm**

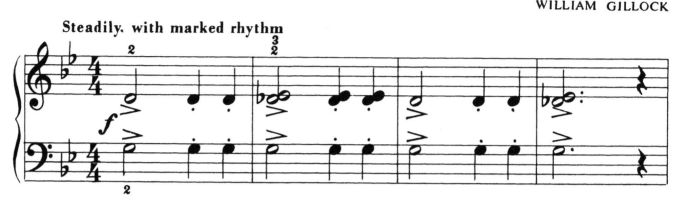

# CLOWNS

WILLIAM GILLOCK

**Rather fast, humorously**

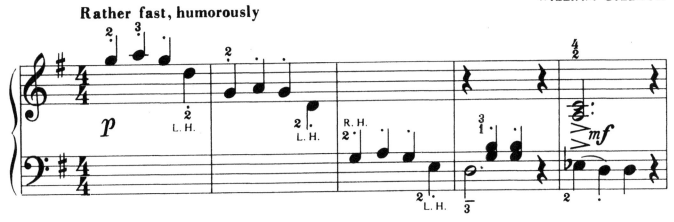

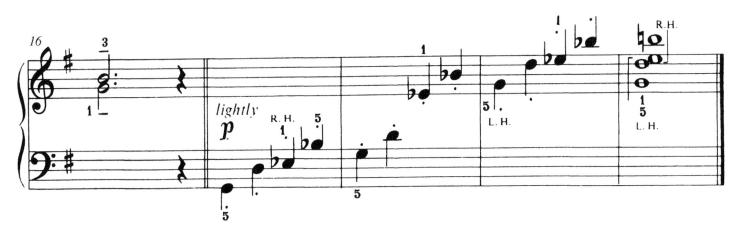

# PAGODA BELLS

WILLIAM GILLOCK

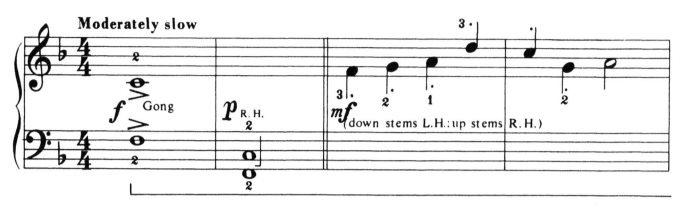

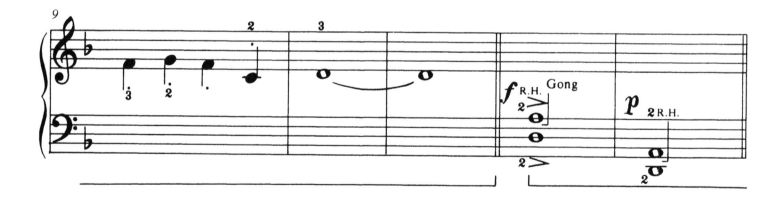

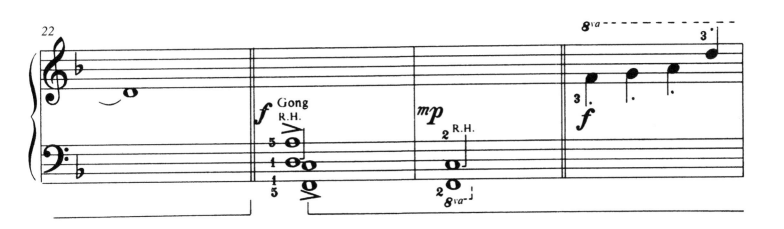

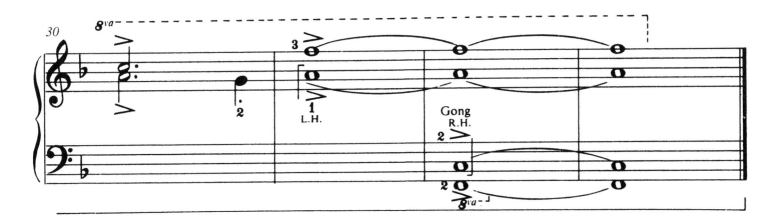

# THE LITTLE SHEPHERD

WILLIAM GILLOCK

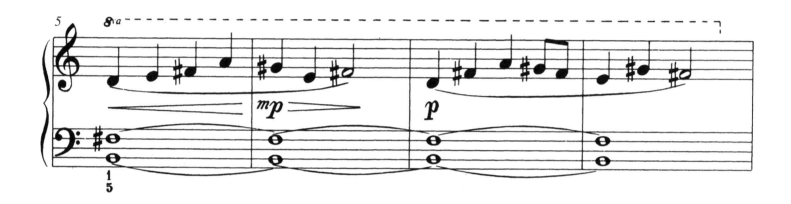

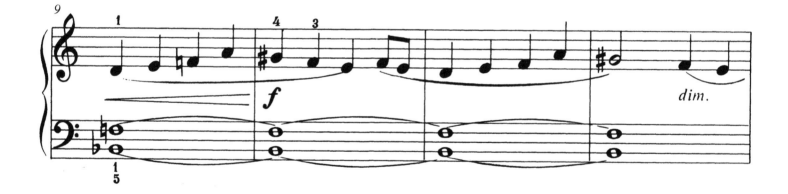

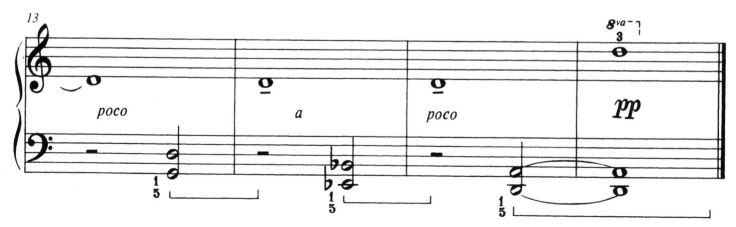

# WATER LILIES

WILLIAM GILLOCK

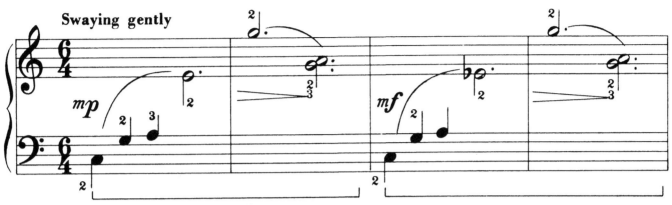

( Up-stems R.H.; Down-stems L.H. )

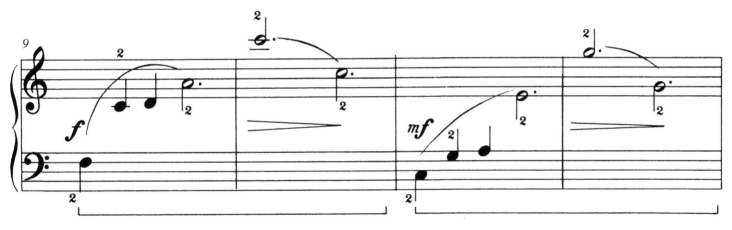

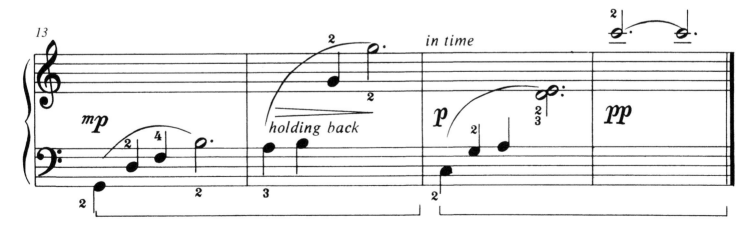

# SWING YOUR PARTNER

WILLIAM GILLOCK

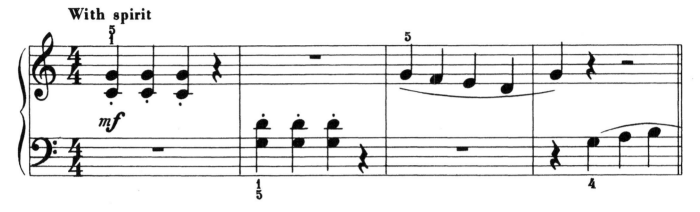

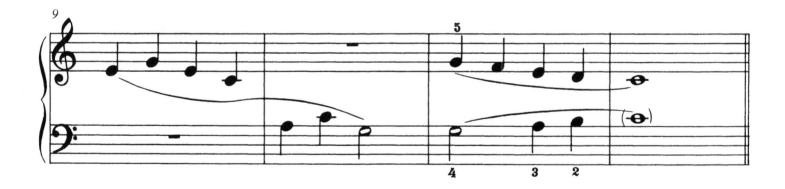

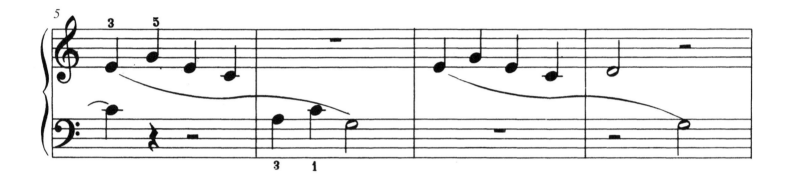

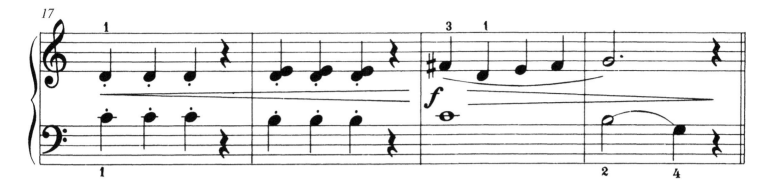

# SPOOKY FOOTSTEPS

WILLIAM GILLOCK

**Slowly, mysteriously**

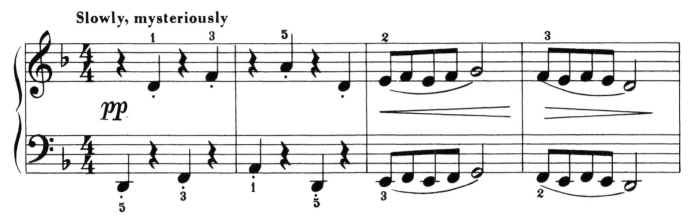

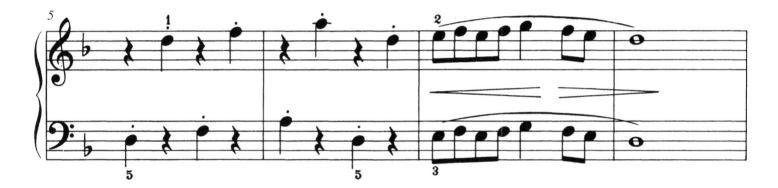

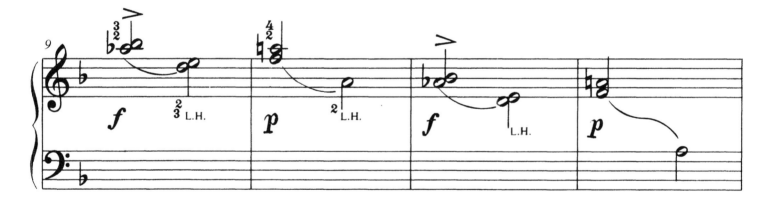

# NEW ROLLER SKATES

WILLIAM GILLOCK

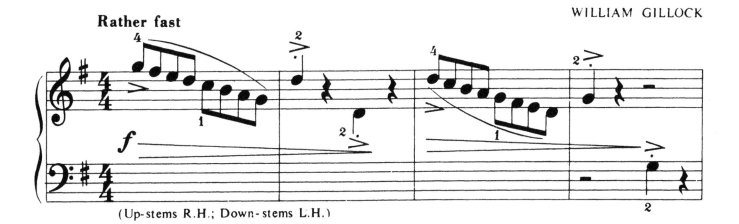

**Rather fast**

*f*

(Up-stems R.H.; Down-stems L.H.)

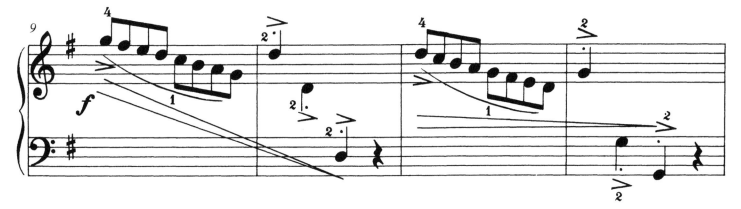

*p*

*cresc.*

*f*

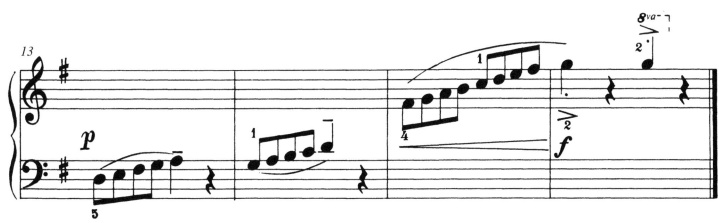

*p*

# THE GLASS SLIPPER

WILLIAM GILLOCK

**In waltz time**

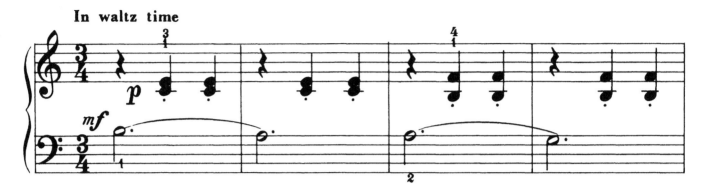

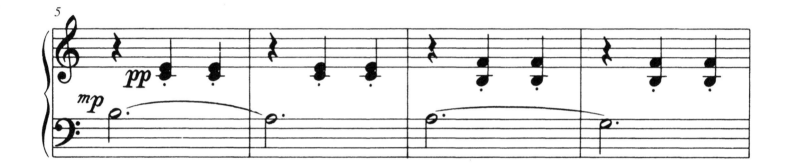

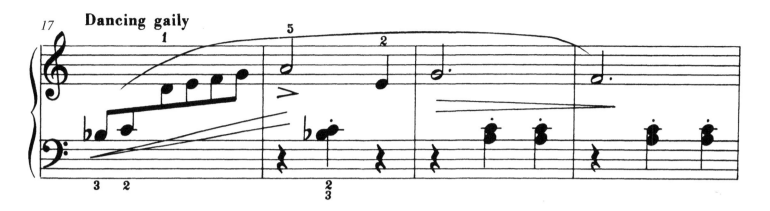

Dancing gaily

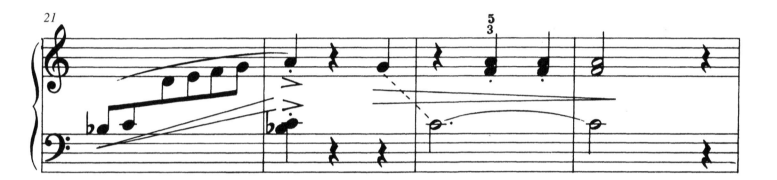

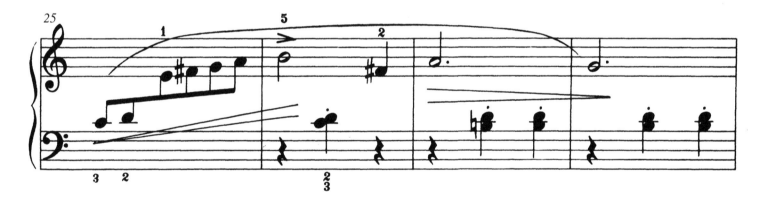

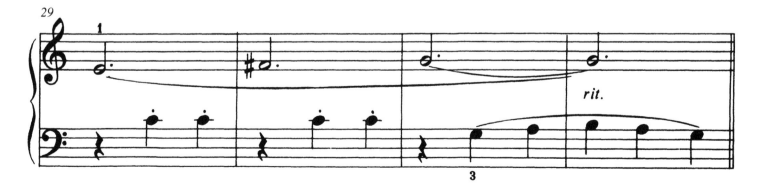

*rit.*

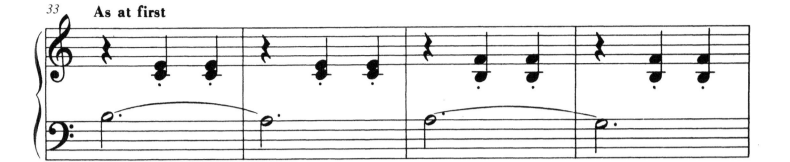

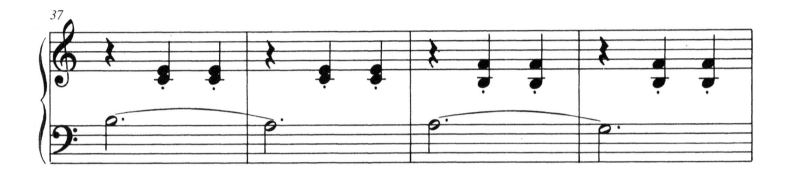

Cinderella runs away_____ losing her slipper!